It's a Banner Year!

George Collopy

Published by **Resource Publications, Inc.,**
160 E. Virginia St. Suite 290, San Jose, CA 95112

Editorial Director: Kenneth Guentert
Design: George Collopy
Production Editor: Kathi Drolet
Mechanical Layout: Terri Ysseldyke-All

Library of Congress Cataloging-in-Publication Data available
ISBN: 0-89390-176-8

**"The art
of our own days
coming from
every race and region
shall be given
free scope
in the Church."**

Environment and Art in Catholic Worship
published by the National Conference of Catholic Bishops

CONTENTS

Introduction

Since this is a *how-to* book about *no-word* banners, the introduction will be a succinct one. Simply, the following designs are to be only a direction. Don't copy them slavishly; use the designs as a springboard for your own creativity. Adapt them to your own environment: change the proportions, make them mini or maxi, create your own textures, patterns and color combinations to contrast or complement the surroundings. Since we've had a plethora of banners with words, here's an opportunity for you to invoke a *feeling* in your congregation without the use of the alphabet. If you're hesitant about your design ability, lean on the golden rectangle from the *The Geometry of Art and Life* (see Bibliography on pages xiv-xv) for moral support. Consider using the designs that follow for lobby areas, processions, and other functions as well. Also, many of the designs have counterparts based on the church year in *Clip Art for Bulletins and Beyond* which can be adapted to children's liturgies, mini-banners, etc. For example, the Jesse Tree (the opening banner in this book), has twenty-five spot drawings which can be adapted to either mini-banners or several walls of individual designs.

Get It Off The Ground

Read the paperback on *Environment and Art in Catholic Worship*. It espouses the cause of the artist and states that the art consultant should be an integral member of the liturgy commission. It reaffirms that the "art *of our own days* coming from every race and region, shall be given free scope in the Church..." (p.9). You can't find a better starting point.

Make It Bigger

There are a number of ways to quickly and accurately enlarge a piece of clip art.

Reproductive stats, for preparing artwork for printing, are available at quick-print shops and are priced according to size.

Opaque projectors, available in all schools will project flat artwork onto a vertical surface for retracing.

Overhead projectors will do the same as above, except that you will have to transfer your original piece of art to clear acetate before projecting.

Transposing with a grid system is another way to enlarge. Draw a grid system of squares over the original piece of clip art. Use the *same* number of grid squares in the enlarged size you want to reproduce. Working one square at a time, place a dot on each grid line of the enlarged pattern where the design is intersected on the small original pattern. Connect the dots.

You've Got A Friend In Your Copy Machine

Don't overlook the possibilities of using your copy machine as an art tool. Webster defines art as "the conscious use of skill, taste and creative imagination in the practical definition or production of beauty." Use your copy machine to reproduce a piece of "art" in black, a single color, or full color. Assemble the images (combine different ones, or use the same image in a repetitive pattern) on your banner. Glue or tape them together for a paper mural. Explore heat transfers, blueprint machines, and light paintings. Copy on paper, mylar, matte film, or cotton/polyester.

Color It

A few suggestions have been made regarding color, but for the most part you are on your own. It's always best to look at color swatches in the church itself, in both natural and artificial light. This enables you to judge the effect of the color and the light against the surroundings.

The traditional colors used in the church year are: purple for Advent and Lent; white for Christmas and Easter, All Saints (November 1), John the Baptist (June 24), John the Evangelist (December 27), the Chair of Peter (February 22) and the Conversion of Paul (January 25), for the feasts of the Lord (other than the passion) and for feasts of Mary and the saints (other than the martyrs); red for Palm Sunday, Good Friday, Pentecost, celebrations of the passion, birthdays of the apostles and evangelists, and for feasts of martyrs; green is used for ordinary time.

Color restrictions are not as stringent today and I would suggest reaching out for new combinations. See Jim Stockton's *Designer's Guide to Color* for ideas. He has three wonderful paperbacks on color combinations in this series. Also, study the paintings of our modern masters for exciting colors to adapt to your projects. Look to Matisse, Gauguin, Picasso, Stuart Davis, and Joan Miro'. Investigate the innovative uses of color in the folk art of the American Indian, the Eskimo, and of Mexico.

About Chapter Seven

Since church dimensions vary so widely, I can only give you a running start on the approach. However, the topic is worth pursuing if only to get away from the usual 4' x 5' banners flanking the altar. The banners in this book can flank the altar as in *Drape it*, but your project can soar. Look at *Hang an Angel* (p.163), *Bag a Dove* (p.161), and *Catch a Shooting Star* (p.147). Look at the inspirational work of Nancy Chinn (*Modern Liturgy*, 15:6 [cover]; 16:1, p.4). Don't overlook the possibilities of such a spectacular approach. Use the ideas in this section to stimulate your own imagination.

And About Chapter Eight

Unless you have a very progressive congregation, I suggest that you limit most of these designs to your parish hall, gym, or meeting rooms.

Go do it!

VARIOUS SHAPES
AND ARRANGEMENTS

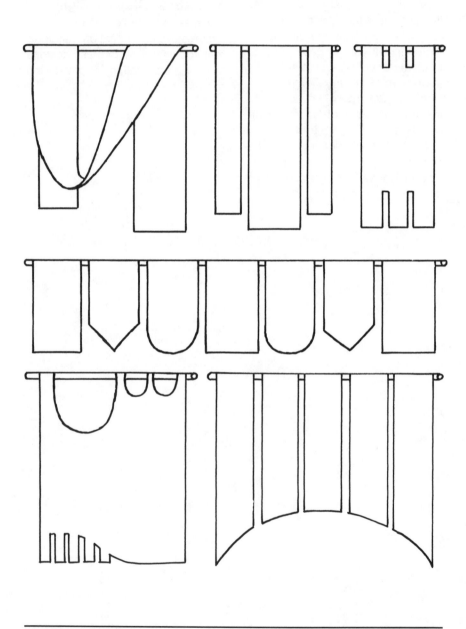

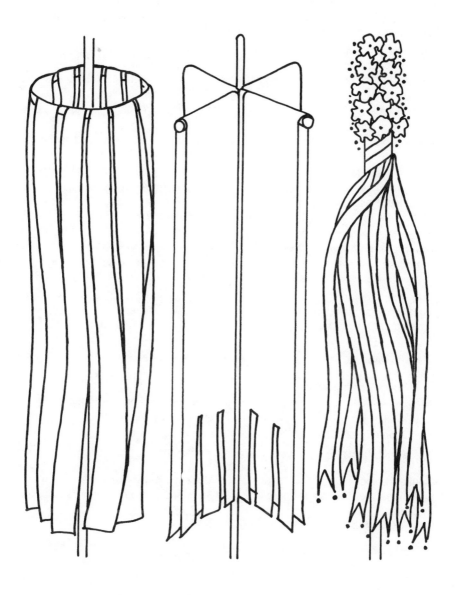

BIBLIOGRAPHY

Bishops' Committee on Liturgy.
*Environment and Art in Catholic
Worship.*
Washington, DC: USCC, 1978.

Blair, Margot Carter.
Banners and Flags.
New York: Harcourt Brace Jovanovich,
1977.

Bradner, John.
Symbols of Church Seasons and Days.
Wilton, Conn.: Morehouse-Barlow
Company, 1977.

Collopy, George.
Clip Art for Bulletins and Beyond.
San Jose: Resource Publications, Inc.,
1988.

Daves, Michael.
*Young Readers Book of Christian
Symbolism.*
Nashville: Abingdon Press, 1967.

Ferguson, George.
Signs and Symbols in Christian Art.
New York: Oxford University Press,
1961.

Firpo, Patrick.
Copy Art.
New York: Richard Marek Publishers,
1978.

Ghyka, Matila.
The Geometry of Art and Life.
Mineola, N.Y.: Dover Publications,
1978.

Gouker, Loice.
*A Dictionary of Church Terms and
Symbols.*
Norwalk, Conn.: C.R. Gibson Co., 1974.

Itten, Johannes.
The Art of Color
New York: Van Nostrand Reinhold,
1973.

Knuth, Jill.
Banners Without Words.
San Jose: Resource Publications, Inc.
1986.

Koch, Rudolph.
The Book of Signs.
Mineola, N.Y.: Dover Publications,
1930.

Krier, Catherine H.
Symbols for All Seasons.
San Jose: Resource Publications,
Inc.,1988.

Laliberté, Norman.
Banners and Hangings.
New York: Van Norstrand Reinhold,
1966.

Laury, Jean Ray.
Applique Stitchery.
New York:Van Nostrand Reinhold,
1966.

Matthews, Wendell.
*Basic Symbols and Terms of the
Church.*
Philadelphia: Fortress Press, 1971.

McLoughlin, Helen.
Family Advent Customs.
Collegeville, Minn.: The Liturgical Press,
1954.

Modern Liturgy Magazine.
San Jose: Resource Publications, Inc.
Ortegel, Adelaide.
Banners and Such.
San Jose: Resource Publications,
Inc.,1986.

Pavey, Donald.
Color.
Los Angeles: The Knapp Press, 1980.

Post, W. Ellwood.
Saints, Signs, and Symbols.
Wilton, Conn.: Morehouse-Barlow
Company, 1962.

Rest, Friederich.
Our Christian Symbols.
Philadelphia: The Christian Education
Press, 1959.

Rockland, Mae Shafter.
The Work of Our Hands.
New York: Schocken Books, 1973.

Sill, Gertrude Grace.
*A Handbook of Symbols in
Christian Art.*
London: Casell & Company, Ltd., 1975.

Stockton, James.
Designer's Guide to Color.
San Francisco: Chronicle Books, 1984.

Whittemore, Carroll E.
Symbols of the Church.
Nashville: Abingdon Press, 1959.

PART

Advent/Christmas
and
Related Feasts

Jesse Tree...one

Use Joseph's Coat as the basis for your Jesse Tree. Divide *coat* into a number of brightly colored squares and superimpose the various symbols. Add pieces of mirror, glass, beads or sequins to hit the light.

An alternate, more conventional approach appears on the following page.

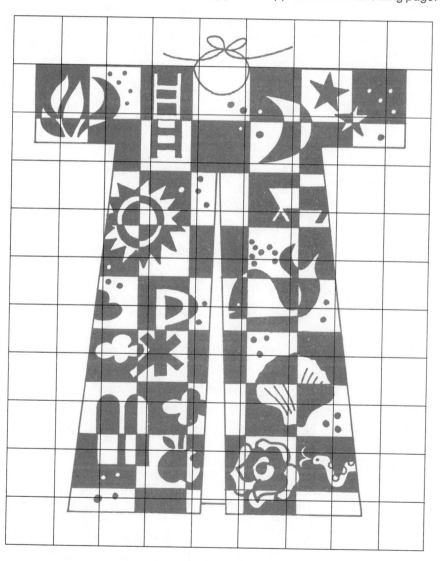

Jesse Tree...another

Isaiah

Consult the readings for the first three Sundays of Advent. Isaiah, and John and Mary (following), will work well either alone or combined as a triptych for the Advent season.

Mary

John the Baptist

Christmas Star...one

The infant Jesus can be portrayed in gold with a contemporary star in shades of red and purple, on a white ground.

Christmas Star...another

Based on an Early American quilt, this design could be fabricated with pieces of patterned material in the traditional manner or in bright, contemporary colors. Study the wonderfully contemporary color combinations of the Amish quilts.

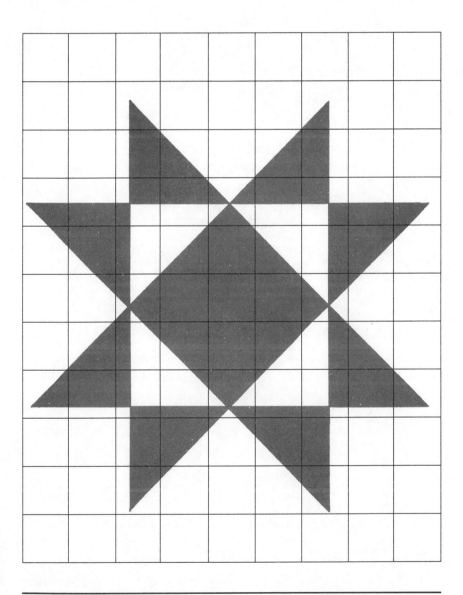

Feast of the Holy Family

The Eighth Day

The official feast for this day is the Solemnity of Mary, Mother of God. It encompasses all of her other feasts and titles. It is also called the "Eighth Day," referring to the seven days of the week plus the one day beyond time, the day of eternity, and the World Day of Prayer for Peace.

Epiphany

The three wise men bear gifts to the Christ Child.

The Baptism of our Lord

PART

Lent/Easter Season
and
Related Feasts

Ash Wednesday

A time of interior conversion. Prayer, fasting, and charitable works start from the heart and they work hand in hand to promote spiritual growth.

Passion/Palm Sunday

Palm branches suggest Christ's triumphal entry, and also direct our attention to the crucifixion.

Holy Thursday

The washing of the feet.

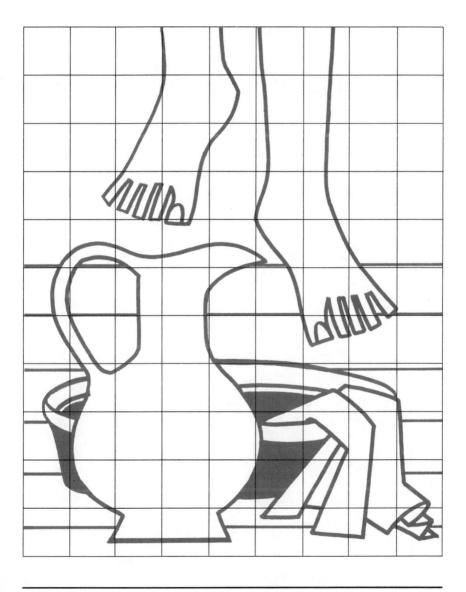

Good Friday

The crucifixion. The rose symbolizes eternal life.

Easter Sunday...one

Consider tacking streamers to the middle-top of the banner, combined with silver seals embossed with the Chi-Rho.

Easter Sunday...another

The butterfly is a traditional symbol of the Resurrection.

Ascension

The ascension of our Lord into heaven. This concept is adapted from a medieval painting.

Pentecost...one

The Holy Spirit with seven flames or tongues which signify the seven gifts.

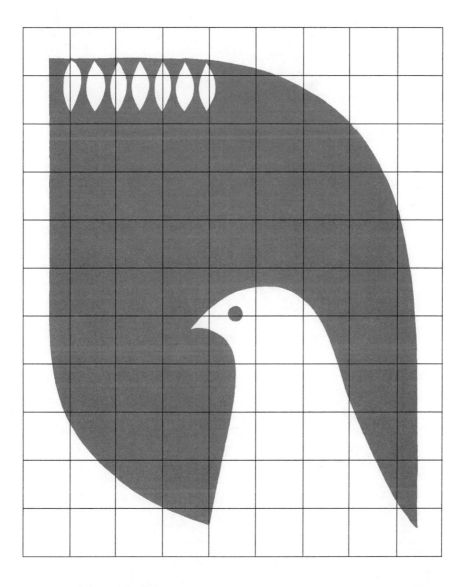

Pentecost...seven

Seven doves representing the Holy Spirit and the seven gifts.

PART

III

Following
Easter

The Holy Trinity...one

The Holy Trinity...another

God the Father, God the Son (the fish), and God the Holy Spirit (the dove).

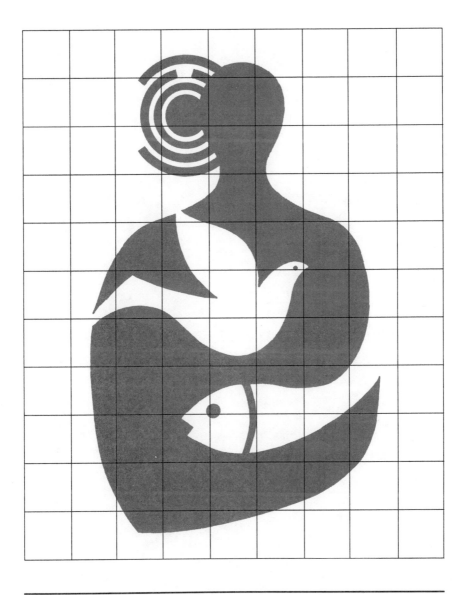

God the Father

God the Son

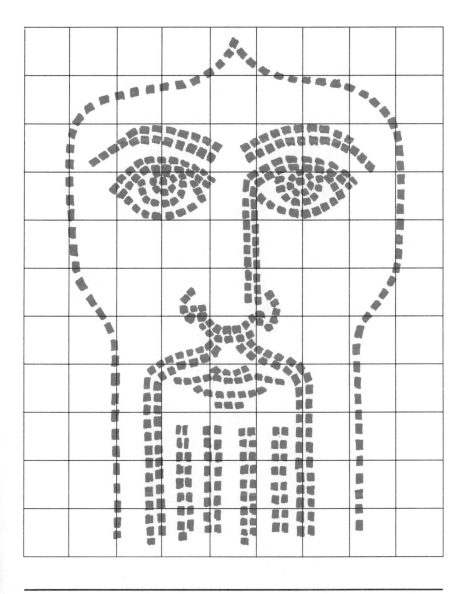

God the Holy Spirit

Try white buttons or silver discs on a dark blue or black ground.

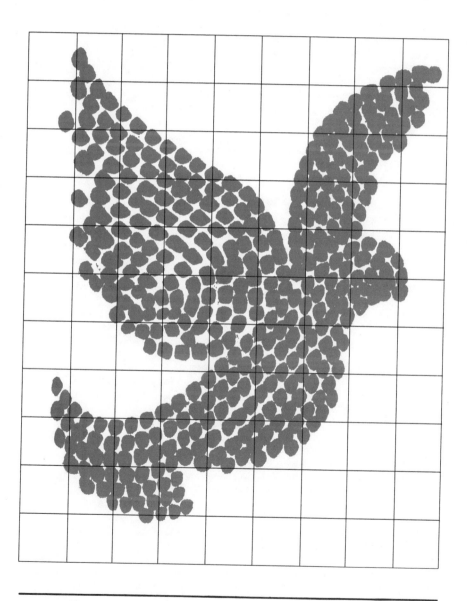

Corpus Christi

The body of Christ, the crucifixion, bread and wine, baptism, and love are all represented.

Sacred Heart

Try a magenta heart on a pink ground with white, three-dimensional flowers.

Christt the King

The sun as a symbol of Christ, is based upon the prophecy of Malachi: "sun of righteousness" (4:2). Use bright oranges, reds, yellows, and metallic golds. Sew or glue sequins, mirrors, and jewels to catch the light. Use gold mylar as a background and light the banner with spots to further enhance the brilliance.

PART

IV

Seasons
of the
Year

Spring

Try a light green background with dark green leaves.

Summer

Use a bright blue background with light green leaves and add white flowers with orange centers.

Autumn

Make a light brown tree with gold, red, and brown leaves.

Winter

Complement the white tree with a royal blue background.

PART

Other
Feasts

Presentation

Although the previous Holy Family banner (Part I, p.17) would be appropriate for this feast, consider the theme, "Christ is the light of all the people." Use a sheer material or mylar with the Chi-Rho symbol and shafts of light in gold and silver. Spotlight.

Saint Joseph

Annunciation...one

The encounter of Mary with the angel. The lily is a traditional flower for the Mother of God.

Annunciation...another

The angel, alone, but consider bright reds, pinks, and purples.

John the Baptist

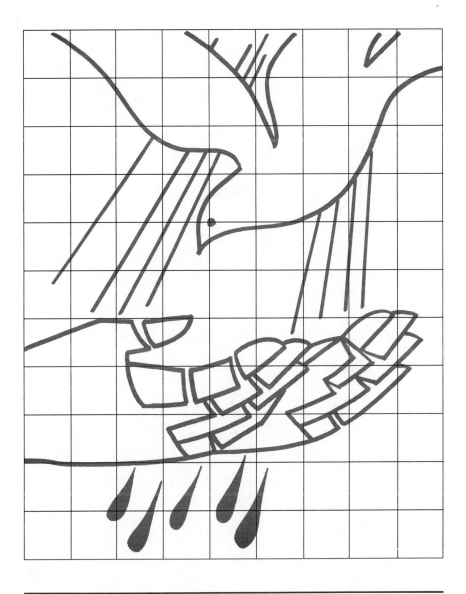

Saint Peter

The crossed keys are symbols of Peter's authority.

Saint Paul

Paul is often represented by the sword and the scriptures.

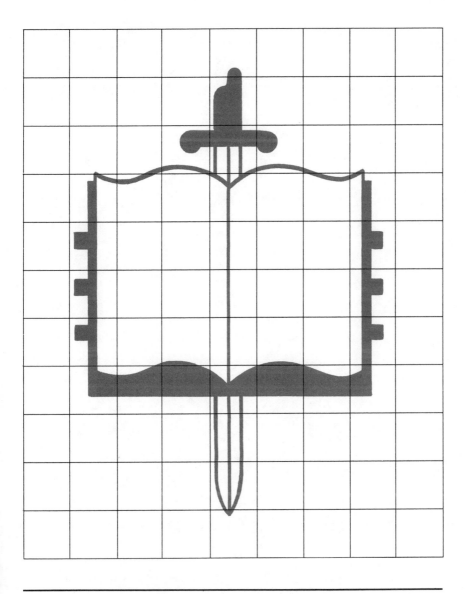

Transfiguration...one

Transfiguration...another

Assumption...one

The bodily assumption of Mary into heaven.

Assumption...another

Mary represented as the Queen of Heaven.

Triumph of the Cross

Try a white cross on a bright red ground with yellow, orange, and magenta radiants.

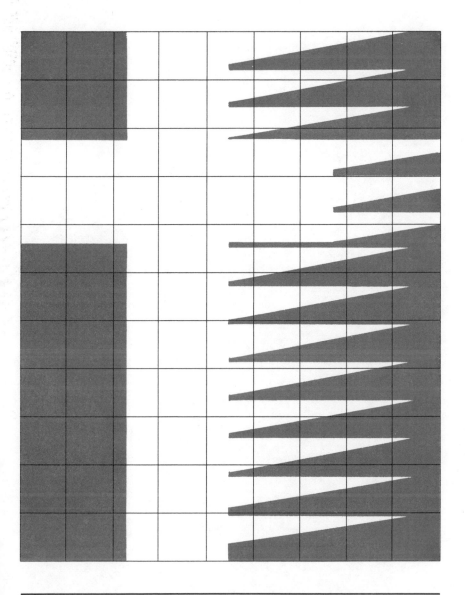

All Saints

All Souls

Saint John Lateran

Whenever All Souls Day falls on a Sunday, the following Sunday celebrates the feast of the Dedication of the Basilica of St. John Lateran. This basilica is the cathedral of Rome, the Pope's own church, and the mother of all churches throughout the world. The beehive is an ancient symbol for the Church.

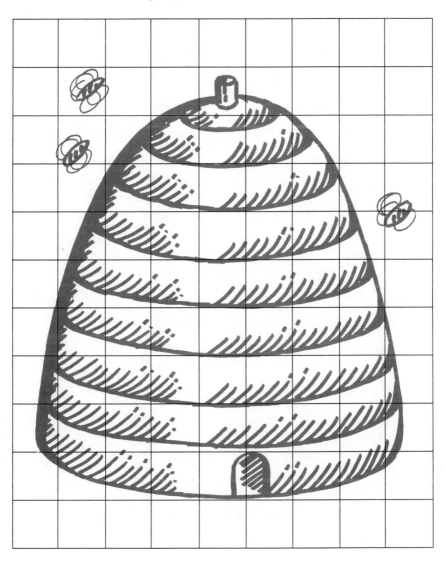

Immaculate Conception

PART
VI

Sacraments

Baptism

Reconciliation

Confirmation

Divide the banner into quarters. On the top half, use orange and red; on the bottom, light and dark blue. Make the dove in white, and try hot pinks, oranges, and reds for the seven flames.

Communion

This banner can be produced as a simple silhouette, or in a mosaic pattern using browns and tans for the bread, and magentas and purples for the wine.

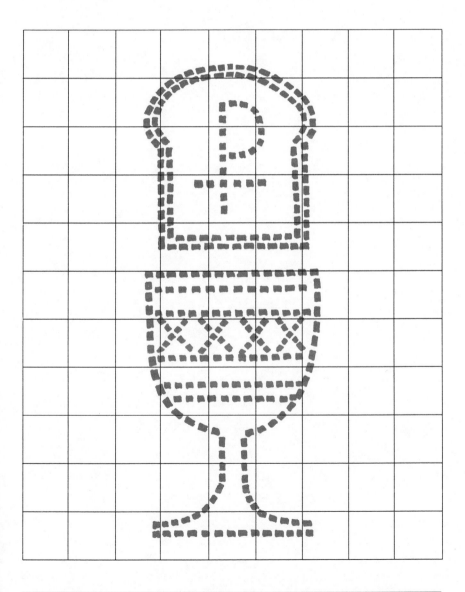

Matrimony

Holy Orders

This is a priest's coat of arms derived from early ecclesiastical heraldry. Update it by using a bold black outline on a brightly colored ground.

(An alternative to the fisherman's net described in Part VII, p. 151.)

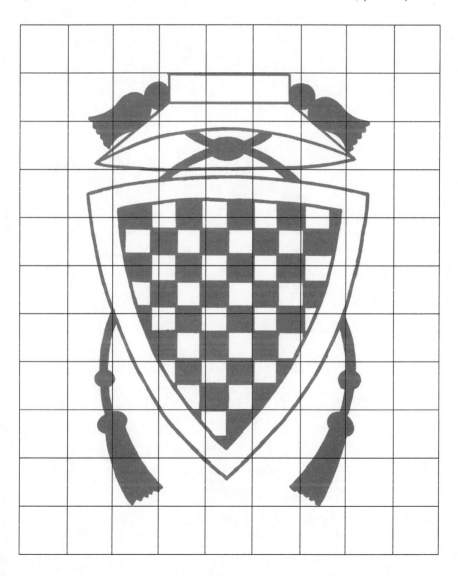

Anointing

PART

VII

New
Directions

About Face

Photocopy various reproductions of the the faces of Christ, the Blessed Mother, or your favorite saint. For interest, select pictures done in different media (e.g., combine line drawings with washes and with paintings). Crop the copies tightly and assemble them into a modular collage.

Collage Try

Paint or construct a large collage in a variety of colors. Cut the collage into squares or rectangles and reassemble the pieces into a new, random pattern.

Found Objects

Fill heavy-duty plastic bags with found objects (e.g., pressed flowers, mounted butterflies, shells, etc.).

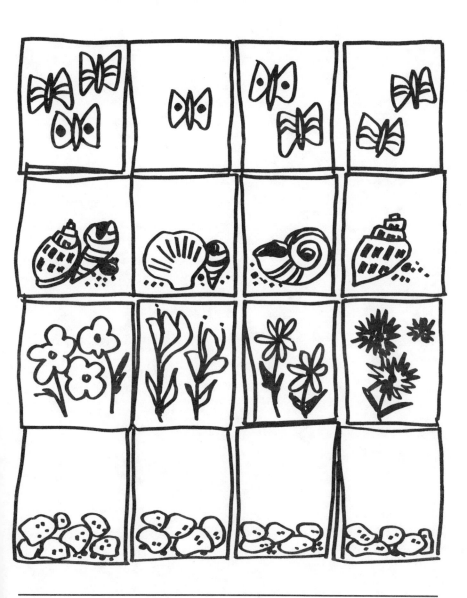

More Found Objects

Make a banner out of found objects. For this banner, use painter's gloves dyed in pastel colors. Sew the gloves together in an all-over pattern. *Hands to work...hearts to God*?

Saint in 1-D

For your special Saint Day, cut a one-dimensional figure out of foam core. Photostat an old engraving to size for the face and then paint the remainder of the figure. Support the figure with a triangular base and place it in the altar area. A two-dimensional addition (e.g., the dove in this illustration) will give more interest.

Saint in 3-D

An alternative to the previous *Saint Day in 1-D* project is to use a stack of white boxes with the saint's image drawn or painted on the box front. Offset the boxes for a more interesting effect.

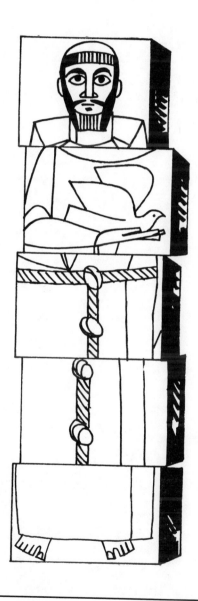

Homage to Calder...one

Flank the altar with an interpretation of Alex Calder's *stabiles*: stationary sculpture made from foam core. Paint the sculpture in monochromatic tones to fit the setting or to fit the occasion; or, make it wild and exciting with bright colors and Jackson Pollack drippings.

Homage to Calder...better one

Try a mobile suspended from a light-weight pole. Each panel can revolve independently. Use different colors, or design an over-all pattern and cut the foam core into five separate pieces.

Hang-up

Make garlands of *over-sized* fabric flowers linked together with other fabrics. Use satins, metallics, etc., and color them to the season.

Up in the Clouds

Suspend clouds of foam core with transparent fishing line. As an alternative, use chicken wire stuffed with cotton or pompoms of crepe paper. (This idea could be used for the feast of the Ascension.) Add streamers of rainbow-colored crepe paper to move with the air.

Stars Above

Cover a cardboard or foam core star with foil and suspend it from the rafters (or cross wires). Use the star singly, or make a group of them. Add colored streamers that move with the currents of the air.

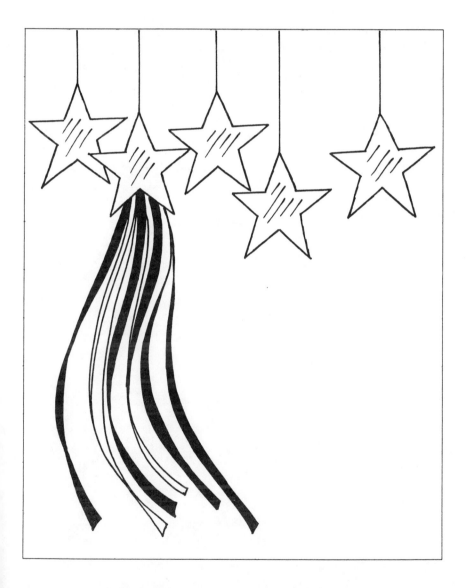

Catch a Shooting Star

Make a *shooting* star of foil-covered foam core with foil or colored streamers. Suspend the star from the ceiling with transparent fishing line.

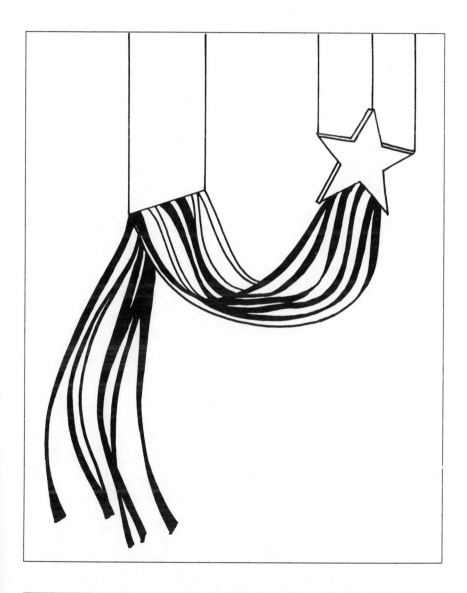

An Early American

Trade in on our early American heritage. Tie leather, and fabrics of turquoise and rust into a swag, using Indian beads and leather thongs decorated with feathers.

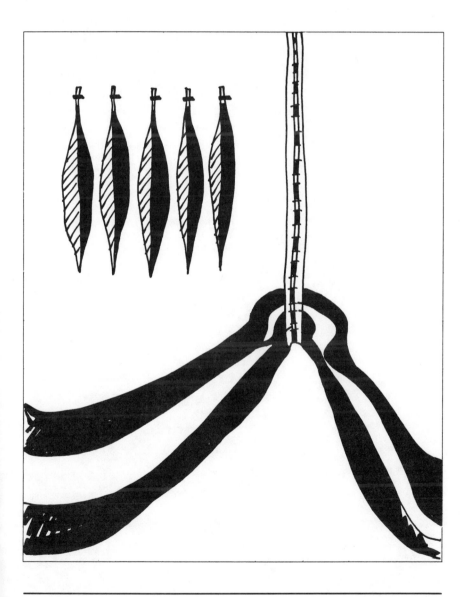

Catch a Fish

Loosely drape a fisherman's net (a real net, an old hammock, a macrame net, or knotted strings). Use a piece of fabric behind the net if necessary for clarity and leave a *pocket* at the bottom of the net. Fill the pocket with paper or cloth men, with fish or shells, or with nothing at all.

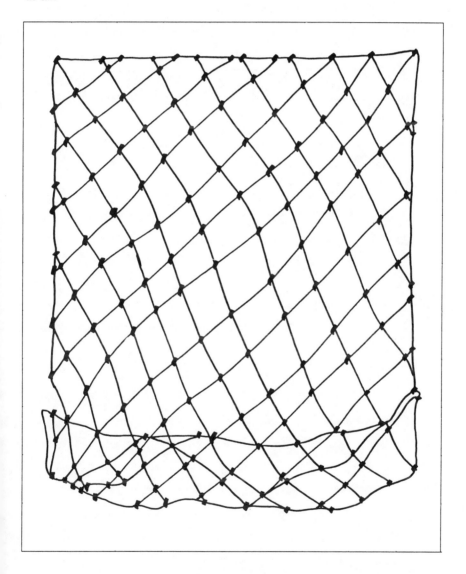

Homage to Hero Miró

Borrow ideas from contemporary artists. This banner, adapted from a collage by Miró , employs yarn, burlap, and other materials.

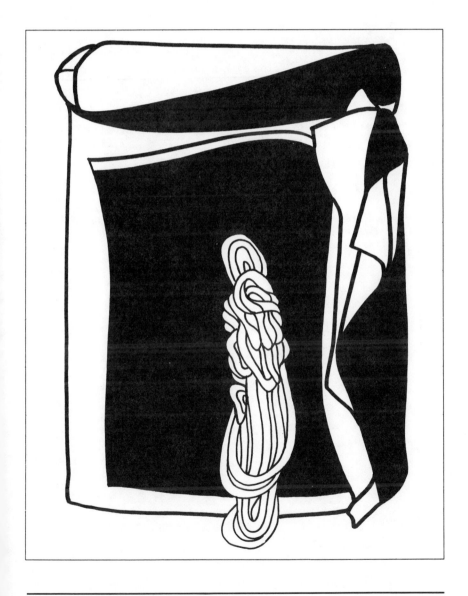

Drape It

Drape different materials: tapestry, woven cloth, textured fabric, transparent fabric. Tie them to create interesting folds. Use colors that key to the feasts and to the church's interior. For example, if the church's statues are monochromatic, drape them with bright colors that correspond to the feast.

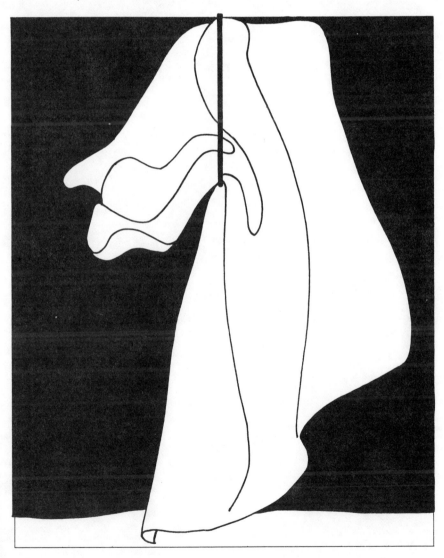

Or-igami

Fold heavy pieces of construction paper origami-fashion. Pierce, then hang them with cord.

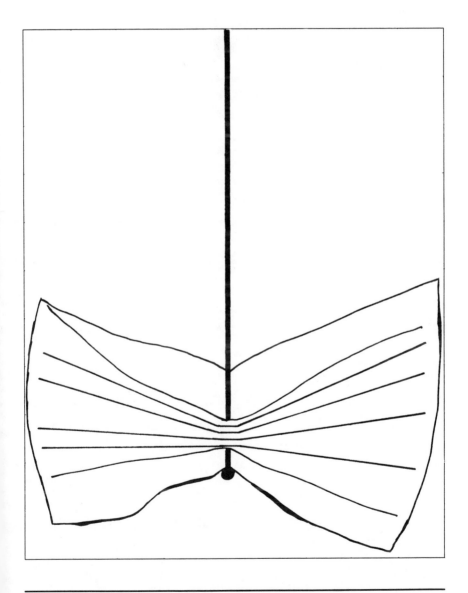

Fly a Kite

Make your own kites or buy them. Use a variety of shapes. Select a special color scheme or mix-and-match. Add tails for motion. Suspend the kites with transparent fishing wire.

Bag a Dove

Using a stuffed pillow case, make a three-dimensional dove to preside over the congregation from the rafters. If possible, use wire on the wings so that they will flap. Add gold rays over the dove's head.

Hang an Angel

Using papier-maché over chicken wire, make a life-size angel. (Or use a life-size mannequin and add wings.) Add feathers to the wings if possible. All white is recommended, with minimal human features. Suspend the angel from the rafters. (Great for the Annunciation and other feasts!)

Soon It's Gonna Rain

Suspend a cluster of umbrellas (rain or beach) for any feast celebrating water.

PART

VIII

Holidays

New Year's Day

Combine one-dimensional balloons made of fabric with confetti and spiraling ribbons. Tack the ribbons to the top of the banner to move freely in the breeze.

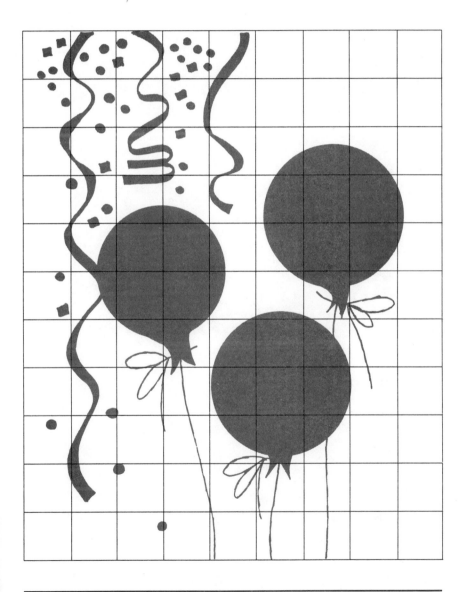

Martin Luther King Day

On the left side, make the hair blue with white stars, and the face brown. On the right side, use red and white stripes, and make the face cream-colored.

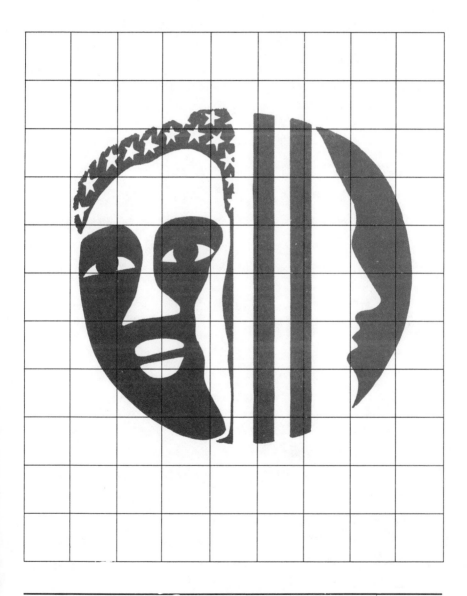

Lincoln's Birthday

Make Lincoln's stove pipe hat black. Use a blue ground for white stars and stripe the rest of the banner in red and white.

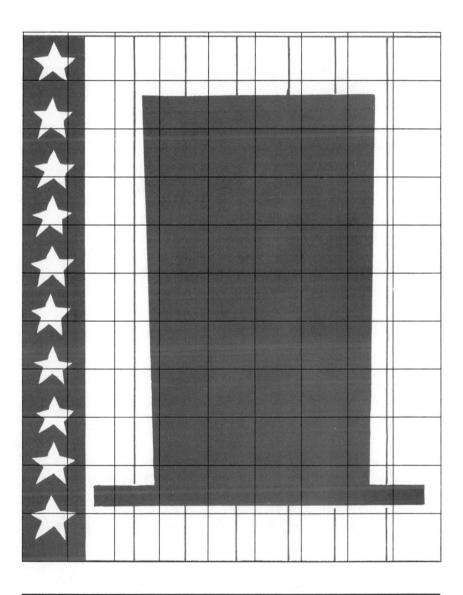

George Washington's Birthday

Use pink or light green for the top stripe. Add red cherries with green stem. Make George's face and the background in black.

Valentine's Day

Saint Patrick's Day

Orange and green are the colors of the Irish flag, so it is perfectly permissible to use a green shamrock on an orange ground. Try an individual shamrock, an over-all pattern, or use the shamrock with the Celtic derivation shown here.

April Fool's Day

Suggest a clown using black shapes and the traditional clown's make-up. Use bright colors for the patterned gloves. A fool for Christ?

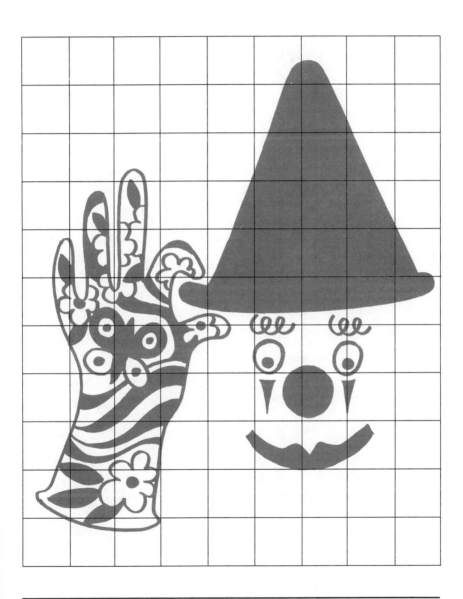

Passover

Pesach (or Passover) celebrates the Israelites' freedom from the Egyptians. The traditional Passover meal consists of wine, matzot, bitter herbs, charoset, vegetables, and on the dinner plate, a roasted bone as a reminder of the sacrificed lamb.

Mother's Day

The traditional carnation is used in this banner. A red carnation symbolizes true love and a pink carnation is the symbol of marriage.

Flag Day

Honor the various ethnic groups in your congregation by displaying flags from each of their countries. It is best to make the flags so that all of them will be the same size and texture. Consult an atlas for reference and be certain to hang them in the correct manner.

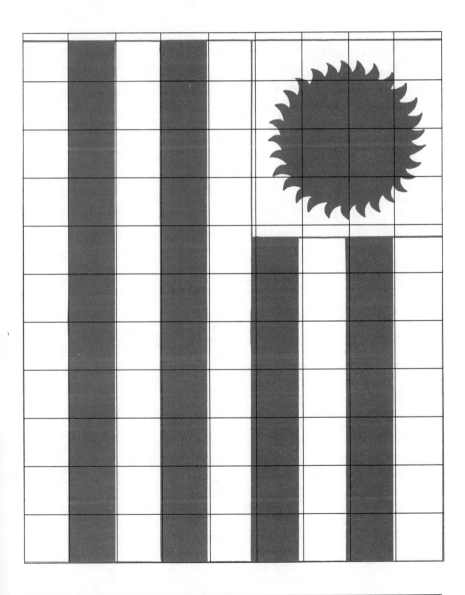

Father's Day

The traditional necktie is used in this banner. It is accompanied by a gift of love.

Independence Day

With a navy blue background, simulate fireworks using magentas, pinks, reds, and yellows.

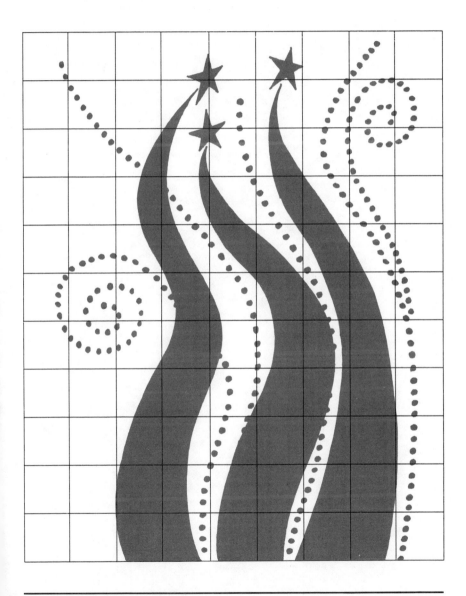

Friendship Day

Usually celebrated near the Fourteenth Sunday of Ordinary Time, this banner helps us to remember the friends we have and those on whom we depend.

Labor Day

The traditional symbol of labor, the arm and hammer, is combined with the dove to remind us of God's blessing on our work. It also signifies that labor is derived from the power of God.

Grandparents' Day

Rosh Hashanah

The Jewish New Year begins in the fall with Rosh Hashanah. On this feast's second day, the *shofar* (a ram's horn) is blasted thirty times as a reminder of the moment at Sinai when the people accepted the covenant.

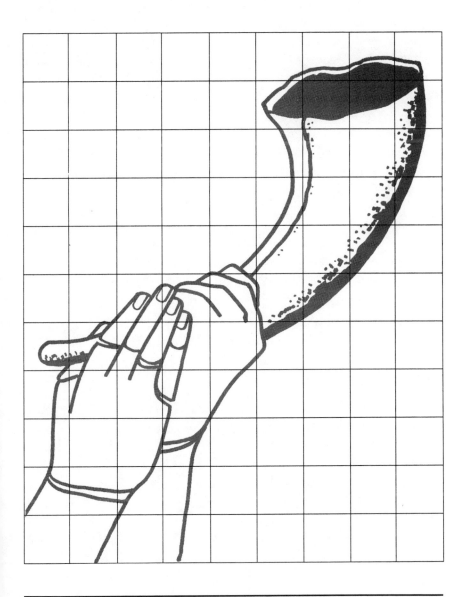

Yom Kippur

On Rosh Hashanah God opens the Book of Life and for ten days studies each person's deeds. Then on Yom Kippur, the holiest of days, God closes the book and decides each person's future.

Columbus Day

Alternate shades of blue and green for the water. Make white sails, black boats, and an orange sun.

Halloween

The traditional black cat is this holiday's symbol. Try green eyes and an orange witch's hat.

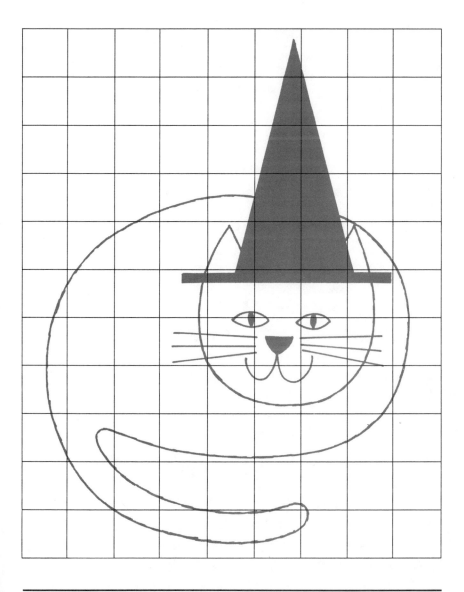

Veteran's Day

Make a variety of banners using only portions of the flag's design, similar to the one illustrated here. For example, make one with horizontal stripes alone, and another with stars alone. If your congregation will tolerate it, try an alternate color scheme. See artist Jasper Johns' renditions of the flag in orange and green.

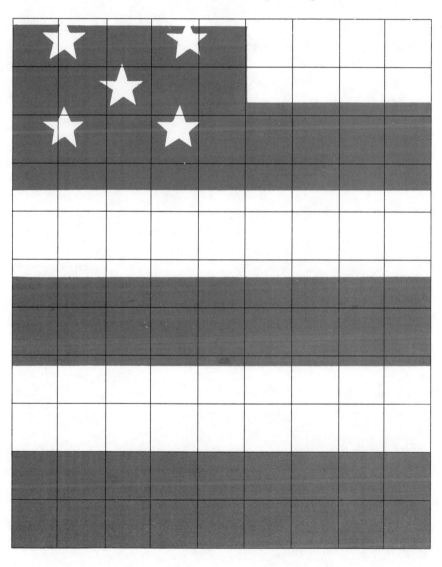

Thanksgiving

Instead of the usual horn of plenty, try Della Robbia swags of leaves, fruit, vegetables, and flowers. Use real or artificial. As an alternative, make this design in felt.

Hanukkah

Hanukkah, a feast of light, celebrates the kindling of fire at the rededication of the Temple altar during the time of the Maccabees. The menorah has eight branches, one of which is lit by a *shammash* (another candle) each day of this eight-day festival.

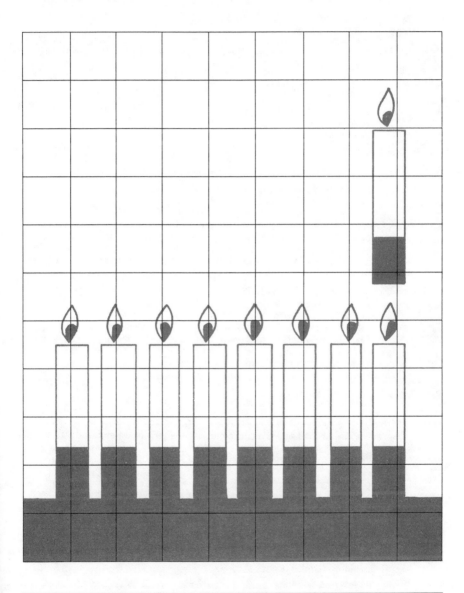

Take the "Plain" Out of "Plain and Simple" with these *Environment Resources:*

BANNERS WITHOUT WORDS
by Jill Knuth
Paperbound $10.95, 198 pages, 6" x 9"
ISBN 0-89390-075-3
This collection of design ideas, illustrations, instructions, and handy tips will help you make your own beautiful, wordless banners. More than 50 reproducible designs!
"An interesting sense of symbolism...fresh images...Incorporates many innovative techniques." — Provident Book Finder

BANNERS AND SUCH
by Adelaide Ortegel, S.P.
Paperbound $10.95, 127 pages, 7" x 10", ISBN 0-89390-092-3
A basic source of design principles for any visual construction—banners, altar cloths, vestments, antependiums, and other creative visual articles. Revised edition includes new section on environments and updated resource guide.

LIGHT: Multimedia Techniques for Celebration
by Adelaide Ortegel, S.P., and Kent E. Schneider
Paperbound $10.95, 144 pages, 7"x 10", ISBN 0-89390-094-X
Light up your next gathering! All you need is a slide projector or overhead—and *Light: Multimedia Techniques for Celebration.* Learn how to make your own slides out of paint, acetate, or contact paper, how to create wonderful fluid effects with an overhead, how to use dissolve techniques, and how to operate two or more projectors at the same time.

SYMBOLS FOR ALL SEASONS:
Planning Worship Environments for Cycles A, B, and C
by Catherine H. Krier
Paperbound $9.95, 175 pages, 5½" x 8½", ISBN 0-89390-125-3
Chock-full of symbols based on the Sunday lectionary readings for all three cycles, this book also gives you tips on liturgy planning, artistic considerations, and color. Includes space to jot down your own ideas.
"A well-thought out celebration of creating a worship experience on a three-dimensional level. Krier nurtures a healthy desire to create a backdrop that will enhance 'the greatest story ever told.' " — Sacramental Life

ORDER FORM --
Ask for these books at your local dealer, or complete the order form below and send it to:

Resource Publications, Inc.
160 E. Virginia Street, Suite 290
San Jose, CA 95112-5848

Qty	Title	Price	Total

☐ My check or money order is enclosed.
☐ Charge my ☐Visa ☐MC Exp. date: _____

Card No. _____-_____-_____-_____

Subtotal _____
California residents add 6¼% sales tax _____
*Postage & handling _____
Total amount enclosed _____

Signature _____

Name: _____
Institution: _____
Street: _____
City: _____ State_____ Zip_____
Code:BY

*Postage & handling
$1.50 for orders under $10.00
$2.00 for orders of $10.00-$25.00
9% (max. $7.00) of order for orders over $25.00

OTHER ART IDEAS

Clip Art for Bulletins and Beyond
by George F. Collopy
Paperbound $14.95, 144 perforated pages, 8½" x 11"
ISBN 0-89390-124-5
Produce easy-to-do, eye-pleasing bulletins, banners, and programs with art appropriate for any Sunday of the liturgical year and in various sizes for your convenience. Learn how to use clip art to your best advantage, how to make different bulletins using different folds, and how to enlarge the art to your specifications.

Clip Art for Communicating the Good News
Jean Morningstar
Paperbound, $14.95, 128 pages, 8½" x 11" perforated
ISBN 0-89390-160-1
Enhance your printed message with this original clip art. These drawings illustrate passages from the Bible, and they cover the seasons of Advent, Christmas, Lent, Easter, Pentecost, and many other feasts. The unique format allows you to use them "as is" or in your own designs. Great for stationery, newsletters, student handouts, Sunday bulletins, and flyers.

"The artistic drawings and calligraphy of Sr. Jean Morningstar are a wonderful blend of simplicity and inspiration. I have used her work in school newsletters, invitations, liturgical program booklets, and stationery...in all cases her work is striking and adds greatly to the material." — Br. Frederick Dihlmann, FSC, St. Joseph's Collegiate Institute, Buffalo, NY

Making Art Together Step-by-Step
by Herb Perr
Paperbound, $12.95, 139 pages, 5½" x 8½"
ISBN 0-89390-118-0
This book guides you step-by-step through 24 easy-to-do projects designed to give students exposure to various art forms from chalk art on the sidewalk to their own videotaped television shows.

"This book fills a vacuum in art education literature. I highly recommend it for elementary and secondary school art teachers, art specialists, and college art educators." — George York, Art Education Consultant, School Arts

"Herb Perr's guide is a contribution to the collaborative approach, giving concrete ideas, methods, and classroom projects...A 'socially concerned' philosophy of art." — NYSATA News

---

Order Form --
Ask for these books at your local dealer, or complete the order form below and send it to:

Resource Publications, Inc.
160 E. Virginia Street, Suite 290
San Jose, CA 95112-5848

Qty	Title	Price	Total
___	_____	___	___
___	_____	___	___
___	_____	___	___

Subtotal _____

California residents add 6¼% sales tax _____

*Postage & handling _____

Total amount enclosed _____

☐ My check or money order is enclosed.
☐ Charge my ☐Visa ☐MC   Exp. date: _____

Card No. _____-_____-_____-_____

Signature _____

Name: _____

Institution: _____

Street: _____

City: _____ State ____ Zip_____

Code:BY

*Postage & handling
$1.50 for orders under $10.00
$2.00 for orders of $10.00-$25.00
9% (max. $7.00) of order for orders over $25.00

INCLUDE THE ARTS IN YOUR PLANNING WITH *MODERN LITURGY*

MODERN LITURGY
for the Artist and Planner

Modern Liturgy is the only liturgical resource devoted to planning worship with help from all of the arts. If you're trying to blend the musical, lively, and environmental arts into your parish worship, this is your magazine! Every issue contains ideas for dramas, stories, gestures, songs, decoration, and design— all in plenty of time for your seasonal planning. Make it easy on yourself: Get a subscription today!

One year (ten issues): $40

Order Form ---

☐ YES, I would like to start receiving the creative ideas of top liturgists from around the world. Rush me my first issue of *Modern Liturgy* and reserve my one-year subscription (10 issues for $40.00). If I'm not satisfied, I can return the invoice marked "cancel" and *keep my first issue free.*

Name: _____

Institution: _____

Address: _____

City/State/Zip _____

Code: